CW01264081

A CELEBRATION OF ENCHANTMENT

The Unique Dolls of Lynne & Michael Roche

Written by Barbara Spadaccini-Day

The present, always linked to the past, is a bridge to the future.

Grateful acknowledgements are
made to the following for their
permission to be quoted:

Patricia Adams

Robin and Charlotte Cooke

Rudolf Ebeling

Estelle Johnston

Antoinette de Rohan

Danny and Barrie Shapiro

To Ian Pout of Teddy Bears
of Witney for the use of his
photographs

And to those whose
professional assistance made
the creation of this book
possible:

Rod Craig and Emma Whyte
of mccdesign Ltd

Published by Yum-Yum Books

ISBN 0-9550096-0-X

Printed by Hunts, Oxford, UK

CONTENTS

If it surprised me to learn that Lynne and Michael Roche are celebrating twenty-five years of doll making, it surprised me even more to realize that I have known this artistic couple for twenty of those years. My first visit to their studio/shop in Bath was in the spring of 1985, just a few years after they had left antique reproductions behind to devote themselves to creating original porcelain dolls. Since that initial visit and interview, I have followed their quiet steady growth with pleased interest and appreciation. I had the opportunity to interview them a second time, at length, seven years later, for a cover story in Dolls magazine, when they had designed approximately two dozen original dolls. When I asked at that time about their goals for the future, Lynne answered, in her traditionally low-key manner, *"just work and try to do it better and better."*

A retrospective look at their dolls over the past decades is testament to their achievement of this goal. Their carefully constructed dolls continue to subtly develop in richness and integrity, while maintaining their distinct look. The identity of design found in the work of the very best artists has been present in Lynne and Michael's creations from the beginning. In 1992, Lynne described this by saying, *"It's...like handwriting...it's your handwriting."* The deeply collaborative nature of their endeavour means that this singular 'handwriting' is actually a harmonious blend of two individual scripts. The delicate balance this blending requires seems daunting, but for the Roches it has become second nature; they have worked together on every doll from the start.

The understated appeal of their simple yet elegant renditions of children is achieved by the couple's strong artistic foundation, refined craftsmanship and use of natural materials as well as their respectful continuation of fine doll making traditions. Like designers of the past such as Käthe Kruse and Sasha Morgenthaler, the Roches create dolls with contemplative expressions that hold the possibility of many moods. And in the tradition of even earlier French and German doll makers, they have successfully married porcelain heads and hands with wooden bodies to attain expressive and smooth positioning of the figures.

One of the greatest pleasures of Lynne and Michael's dolls are their playful clothing and accessories. Fashioned from antique fabrics, brushed cottons, space-dyed felts and combined in layers of prints and colours, appliquéd with wooden toys or knit flowers or perhaps fetchingly embroidered, the garments are at once nostalgic and contemporary. Consider Laura from 1999, who has an old-fashioned aura yet strikes an unmistakable 2005 silhouette in her seaside ensemble of pale-yellow cropped trousers and cropped sweater with a casual roll neck. The dolls are often charmingly accompanied by hand-knit pets; white poodles and bunnies this year, dark and ginger tabby cats and one of my favourites a little 'sausage' dog last year.

I have greatly enjoyed following Lynne and Michael's ascent to the heights of the doll making field. My admiration for their innate artistic talent, their high level of technical skill and their devotion to fine workmanship grows every year. Each new collection is more pleasing than the last; each year their dolls inspire ever greater visual and tactile delight.

by Krystyna Poray Goddu

HOLLY.

Dolls have been collectors' items for many years, both in Europe and in the United States. This passion has helped preserve some of the finest examples of dolls – antique and contemporary.

France has a long record of collectors. At the end of the 19th century, collections of dolls and toys were formed. It appears that the French preceded the American collectors in this domain, who continued when the French passion for collecting dolls and toys notably weakened.

Several of these early French collections are visible today. One example is the Duchess Herminie de Rohan's fine collection, begun in the late 19th century, open to the public in a specially designed museum in the grounds of the Renaissance family castle in Josselin, (Morbihan, Brittany) France.

Antoinette de Rohan continues the family tradition, adding dolls of quality to the historic collection, and hers is a unique example of a museum in France, with artist dolls on permanent display. She has long recognized the intrinsic value of the Roches creation, and here in the Musée de Poupées in Josselin, you can always admire one, or several, of Lynne and Michael Roches' dolls.

Yesterday's antique doll collectors in America were quite eclectic in the choice of the dolls that they appreciated. Some of the best collections of European dolls are located in America. These collectors of yesteryear behaved differently, they were more interested in the general appearance of the doll, its aesthetic value was essential; numbers, moulds, marks, makers were unimportant factors and not even considered as an

incentive to buy. They bought with their hearts, not with their heads. It was pure pleasure that motivated them.

An interesting parallel can be drawn between yesterday's collectors and those of today, specializing in art dolls and modern creations.

Many of the men and women, in the United States and in Europe, attracted to contemporary artist dolls, rejoin the early collectors, following in their footsteps in collecting with their hearts.

In the late 1980s and early 1990s this new race of collectors started to acquire modern creations, not because they thought they might have a potential of being a financial investment, but because they were drawn to the artist's work. They recognize what the artist is trying to express, because the doll brings forth an emotional response, provoking sensations that they can relate to closely. A doll is infused with mysterious powers of magic that tug at your innermost depths.

Like a book, a doll possesses many facets, it is legible and captivates in various and different ways. Lynne says that there should be room for each onlooker to read in to it what they will.

Similar to a painting, you are immediately aware if you like a doll or not, and for additional appreciation it is three-dimensional. It appeals to several senses. You can touch it, hold it, turn it around, look at it from all angles, play with it, set it up in scenes and create your own personal tableaux and fantasies. The dolls created by Lynne and Michael Roche are vibrant examples of this form of art and fit in with the desire of many collector's to touch and enjoy the playability of the dolls.

Patricia Adams from Tucson, U.S.A. says: *"The qualities I love most about the Roche dolls are their expressions and their seemingly infinite possibilities for posing. Both qualities work to make the dolls more natural and evocative of an individual collector's imagination. Their facial expressions are often wistful – as if the dolls were on the verge of a more pronounced emotion such as laughter or tears, and with a movement as seemingly insignificant as the slightest tilting of a head or the lowering of a chin, I can change a dolls expression from pleased to curious to amused to downright petulant.*

I dress, pose, arrange, and photograph my Roche dolls in a constant search for what I jokingly call 'seasonal realism'. Their pictures adorn my annual Christmas cards to other doll collectors, and the dolls themselves occupy places of

Above, 15th anniversary Katy with tiny Florence

honour among my decorations.

I'm drawn to the Roche dolls on an interesting kind of intuitive, visceral level; and although I can't recall having similar dolls in my childhood, it's as if I've 'known' these dolls for a very long time. My life has been immensely enriched by Lynne and Michael's art."

Akin to the collectors of times gone by, this new generation of collectors, especially Americans, do not limit their passion to what is created on home ground alone. Their eclectic tastes in dolls take them further afield, to the shores of Europe, Japan and England. What could be more English than Hannah, Katy, Heidi, or Jessica and who better to represent Great Britain than the Roches?

Americans have been amongst the first to recognize the inherent qualities of the Roche dolls, granting them a place and permanence in the history of modern doll creation.

In the past, the founding of collections and the awareness of dolls gave rise to another form of direct interest in them – that of creating dolls.

At the beginning of the 20th century several movements of doll creation existed in Europe. These occurred principally in Germany and in France and they lasted for about a decade. Until further information is discovered to refute this, this activity seems to have petered out and creation dwindled in the early 1920s after the end of the First World War. There is a famous exception – the Swiss artist, Sasha Morgenthaler who began making dolls and animals in 1933.

During this early period in Germany, one woman's work stood out. Beginning with the creation of dolls for her own and her friends children, to a production of several hundreds, it was soon apparent that what had started as a handmade one-off child's toy, could grow to be a home industry. With time it became a small specialized industry which is still producing dolls today.

The name of Käthe Kruse is celebrated and familiar to all – collectors, as well as those who create. Her dolls are widely admired and rate highly on the list of important dolls, as well as being amongst those that have been of influenced in some way or other. Their charm is timeless and universal. Look into Lynne's workroom and there on the shelf is an old Käthe Kruse doll. Mention her dolls to other creators, and they will tell of their attraction and of how Käthe Kruse has had a lasting appeal and influence.

These early movements – *Puppenreform* in Germany, *la Renaissance de la Poupée Française* in Paris – were not really organized or structured and quickly disappeared, unlike the ones that developed later in the United States and are still thriving, and those that have followed more recently in England, France and Germany.

Antique dolls Jumeau EJ and Huret

Bath, a city in the county of Somerset.

"A terrestrial paradise of gaiety, with plays, concerts and balls far superior to anything a country town could produce; with crescents and a circus of houses more beautiful than anything in London, and without London's bewildering vastness, noise and dirt...That exciting contrast of town and country, lost now when towns straggle out...was particularly marked in Bath, where Lansdowne Hill rises behind the highest crescent."

Jane Austen, A Biography, by Elizabeth Jenkins, published by Victor Gollancz Ltd, London, 1938

Written more than sixty years ago, this still applies to Bath.

The history of Bath goes back to the time of the Romans, who discovered there, a hot sulphurous spa. More than twenty centuries later, the water is still gushing forth, steaming hot. And you can again line-up in the Pump Room to 'take the waters', as was fashionable in Jane Austen's time.

The harmonious, neo-classical style buildings and the town houses were designed in the 18th century, and most have been preserved. Bath is endowed with a prevailing unity of Georgian architecture and a characteristic golden colour. It is extremely pleasant to walk around its streets. History surrounds, but does not overwhelm, and one feels at home and at ease. It is a real living city and everything is within walking distance.

Then, there are many literary allusions to Bath by famous English writers of the 18th and 19th centuries; such as Henry Fielding, Jane Austen, William Wordsworth, Charles Dickens. The wonderful novels of Jane Austen, champion of the English language, evoke an image of a way of life in Southern England at the beginning of the 19th century.

Lynne and Michael Roche live in Bath and their fine dolls are an excellent introduction to this city.

The Roche dolls are for me irrevocably associated with the material aspect of Bath and the novels of Jane Austen.

Does environment have an influence on creation? In my opinion yes – indirectly and sometimes directly. If you look at antique dolls, it is often very easy to discern their French or German origins, because they have 'that air about them'.

With contemporary creation it is perhaps less easy. But can there be any doubt that the dolls by Héloïse are French; those by Elizabeth Pongratz and Sabine Esche, distinctly German, and those by Ellen Turner, American? Ella Haas's children could only originate from some northern country. The tiny delicate miniature children by Jane Davies and those precise historic characters of Jill Bennett are definitely English.

And those made by Lynne and Michael Roche are pinpointed down to Bath, Great Britain *"where the sun shines but where you still need to wear woollies in the height of summer"* said the late, much missed, John Darcy Noble, in his article on the Roches in Contemporary Doll Collector November 1992.

Would they have made the same kind of dolls if they had remained in London? Maybe not.

Bath is a magic, enchanting place, well worth the excursion if you ever go over to Great Britain. It is but a two hour train journey from London.

Those precious, fascinating facets of dolls! The well-known axiom that dolls lead to everything, proves to be so very true. They open strange, unaccountable doors of knowledge, provoke and inspire various degrees of pleasure, aesthetic and emotional, as well as developing strong bonds of friendship.

....*"Practically none of us start out to be doll artists. Looking back on it, though, it seems that everything we have done has led to this goal. Basically, all of us started out with a love of dolls, or of art, or both."*

Susanna Oroyan, past president of NIADA

Lynne and Michael Roche, two extremely likable people, as different as chalk and cheese but so complementary in their art and life. If one dare pinpoint and characterize them with just one distinctive, personal trait each; Lynne would be distinguished by her melodious 100% English voice, and Michael would be defined by that sharp, piercing look of his dark brown eyes.

Lynne

The Roches are both English, although during his young years Michael, who was born in Redhill Surrey in 1948, lived for some years in Kenya and attended school in a Jesuit college in Rhodesia. Maybe this Jesuit education accounts for his dry sense of humour? And accounting for his photographic talents – he received his first Brownie at the age of eight. From that time onwards, he was never without a camera in his hands. Michael has done all the photography since they started to make dolls.

Lynne was born Mary Lynne Gay in 1949 in Enfield,

Above, left – right, Michael and brother Stephen

Michael with Alice taking photos

Middlesex. Between 1968 and 1976, her life gravitated around the arts. For three years (1968 – 1971) she attended Teacher Training College, her main subject, painting. Then she taught for one year, to discover that this was not her path. From 1973 to 1976 she completed her art studies in the renowned Arts School, Camberwell.

Her speciality is fine arts and she is a painter. She would still paint if the dolls left her time, but as things are, there are few spare moments and her inspiration is entirely directed to creating dolls. The painter in her, perhaps, finds a kind of fulfilment in the illustrations she creates for the children's stories that she writes and in the precise colourful stump-work tableaux that she has began to compose recently.

At this early stage, similar to the majority of doll artists in Europe and in America, nothing in her studies destined her to embark on a career of being a creative doll maker. Her prime interest was figurative oil painting. She worked part-time on various jobs – in Covent Garden, (a love of opera and music, which has never left her) and at the Victoria and Albert Museum in London – in order to fulfil her desire to paint.

Though, can there be something in the family genes? Because Lynne's older brother, Derek Gable, is an

Lynne (front left) with brother Derek (middle back) cousin Sue far right and other cousins

inventor. He lives in the United States, and worked with the Mattel toy firm for many years, knowing well the Handlers, the original owners. In the early days, he developed some of the Barbie accessories.

Nor did Michael have any inkling that some ten years later he would be deeply involved in doll making. He was in the Merchant Navy, and until 1972 travelled around the world.

Then Lynne and Michael met.

Michael was restoring antique furniture – hence his knowledge of wood – when they were introduced by mutual friends and were married quietly in London in 1978.

They share a trait of character that is very English – they both like animals; especially cats.

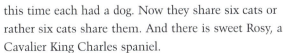

Michael admits to having been very much influenced in his school days by the books of the English zoologist Gerald Durrell, and would have liked to have followed in his footsteps. At this time each had a dog. Now they share six cats or rather six cats share them. And there is sweet Rosy, a Cavalier King Charles spaniel.

Maybe one day, serious research will be undertaken to study the relation and affinities between cats, dolls, collectors, doll makers and artists. The connecting link is possibly aesthetic, contemplative and tactile.

For example in France, Anne Mitrani has a fat, shiny black cat called Rose; Malou, will talk warmly of her close attachment to her cats; Héloïse owns several fluffy tortoiseshell Persians; Rousseau, an elegant Blue Point Siamese, runs the apartment with Barbara. And just one example in the United States is Akira Blount, who is surrounded by the friendliness of an army of cats.

Following her marriage in 1978, Lynne began to deal in textiles and clothes. It was through this connection that she came into contact with antique dolls and Sue Dumper, who had a collection of old dolls. The first attempt to reproduce a doll was with Sue Dumper using a 19th century French E.J. Jumeau.

Lynne's initial knowledge of dolls cames from her attraction and admiration of the antique doll. Her first acquisition was a German Armand Marseille, mould 390, purchased at Bermondsey Market, which with infinite care and precaution she brought back home on her small motorbike. Her love of dolls stems back to childhood, and as young girl she even made clothes for her dolls.

At this date, 1979, the Roches left London and made their home in Bath. Bath was the starting point of a new career and lifestyle. Lynne at first had a booth in the Great Western Antique market on Bartlett Street, selling antique dolls and linen. This incursion into the world of textiles would later serve her well when it came to clothing.

The China Doll

Then at the beginning of 1980, they opened a shop called 'The China Doll' in Walcot Street. The location was ideal, shared by Lynne, now dealing in antique dolls, selling doll's houses and miniatures, and Michael, who was making and fitting kitchen units from the workshop in the rear; hence his experience and skill in the development of the wooden bodies that the majority of their dolls have.

Antique dolls were already popular and much sought after in Great Britain. In the 1970s their prices escalated.

Bored by just dealing in dolls and realizing the potential in making and selling reproductions to those collectors who could not afford to buy an expensive original, Lynne

AT original and copy

ventured into a new domain. For this, during a short period of time, she used the moulds of the American company Seeley – in particular the SFBJ 236 and the 252 Pouty and the Jumeau 'long face' models. Then she began

her personal experience by making trial copies using three of her own dolls; two of which were a 'tête Jumeau' and a wonderful, but cracked A.T., both much sought after late 19th century French dolls.

They were fortunate to have the premises of 'The China Doll' with its adjoining workshop, Michael's domain, in which they installed a small kiln for firing the porcelain. And so they embarked upon a new adventure in the early months of 1980. They had their first orders from Lillian Middleton, an English dealer and from Dov Sagiv in Switzerland. In 1981 they joined The British Toymakers Guild and received their first orders from Granpapa in Japan.

For a short period they made reproductions of the classical French and German bébés. Michael cast the heads, they were fired, painted by Lynne who wigged and dressed the dolls and they were sold from the shop. Michael had not yet attempted to make bodies and

Copies

these heads were assembled on bodies bought from various companies.

They were both dissatisfied with this type of mass produced body and consequently Michael tried his hand at producing something in his workshop, already well established with the appropriate tools. The idea took root from seeing in an antique shop window an all-articulated wooden lay figure, used by painters, and a source of inspiration for doll makers for several centuries.

And why should not Lynne and Michael Roche try their skills at making dolls themselves? Create their own original dolls? People kept badgering them with that question. Finally when they were 'almost ready', they succumbed and decided to try. It is 1981.

They made an excellent team of expertise, with complementary talents.

Lynne's degree and training in the Fine Arts is not a necessity in the role of creative doll maker, but it is a tremendous asset. Her primary interest, painting, has disciplined her to a global comprehension of the value of ambience, the importance of scale and proportion, colours and textures. Her eye is schooled to a vision of the ensemble. All these are fundamental qualities when making a doll, which is a whole and not just a head, however important this part may be.

Michael, the craftsman and the perfectionist, initiated in the secrets of woodwork and restoring antique furniture, brings precision, experience, patience and a propensity for solving problems, all great advantages in doll making.

It was a challenge that they rose to meet, and from the early 1980s they forged ahead, overcoming difficulties, acquiring technical dexterity. Their talents have matured, transforming, enriching the dolls that they create. Each year they push their limits further and create exciting new models. They have earned a name and proved its worth. They are known internationally and appreciated by both collectors and museums worldwide in France, Japan, America, Germany and Holland.

Rudolf Ebeling from The Hague, Holland, says: *"Did Lynne and Michael realize, years ago when they had their antique shop, starting to make reproductions of antique dolls, that they laid the foundations for their future?*

Rudolf Ebeling

The technical skill it involved, was a perfect educational method, a skill they have carried up to perfection through 25 years of doll making.

Michael improved the body design, Lynne the decoration of the heads and they both learned, through the years, to intensify and vary the expression and beauty of the faces.

What I like most about their art, is the fact that they have always been making dolls in the classical sense of the word. As much as I may admire and love different kind of Art Dolls which are more static, my preference goes to those dolls that are movable and which invite play.

They have never ceased to experiment, making new designs every year, providing them with the most delightful accessories and the loveliest of clothes. It is certain, if Lynne hadn't developed as a doll artist, she would have been a perfect fashion designer, a skill she now indulges on her dolls."

Reproducing dolls, either from existing moulds or going through the various steps of making their own moulds, was soon revealed to be limiting. Lynne and Michael Roche evolved and outgrew the procedure. Intelligent and enterprising, they were inspired to move on. With the technical knowledge gained from this experience and Lynne's artistic talent still untapped, they decided to make their own original dolls.

Lynne chose porcelain as the medium because of her love of the old French bébés and some of the German dolls. She still is, whenever possible, an antique doll collector.

And, in the contemporary doll world, like most of her fellow counterparts, she has a small collection of those artists she most admires and can afford to buy, or sometimes exchange with one of her own.

Amongst her favourites, to cite just a few names; she admires Akira Blount, for *"her innovative extensive use of textiles"*; Ella Haas, for *"the non-sentimental realism of her creations"*; Brigitte Deval, Anne Mitrani and Nancy Whiley, for their *"portraying, each in varying degrees, a personal theatricality"*; Elisabeth Pongratz whose dolls she greatly admires because *"the suggested features allow the collector to formulate his or her own idea of a face on her dolls, and the pared-down extreme simplicity of the head and body to their essential form"*; R.John Wright for *"his wonderful expressive use of felt and the perfect interpretation of the different characters from literature"*; Regina and Abinhavo Sandreuter for their *"top-notch craftsmanship"*, are amongst the other names she cites, all presenting very different facets of doll artistry and denoting the scope of her eclectic tastes.

Before becoming completely involved in porcelain she did try her hand, for more than a year, at making wax-headed babies on cloth bodies. The process was finicky and did not suit her so she did not pursue it further at the time. In 1995, she was again motivated to work in this medium, and created not a baby, but a more mature, tall, 20 inch figure in Juliet, who has a sculpted head and shoulders in poured wax on a cloth body, with wax limbs.

During this early period, Lynne and Michael had great success with their 'Beechy heads' – their own humourous appellation for a primitive type of play doll on a cloth body, with an unsophisticated round turned wooden head, painted simply. Made by Lynne and Michael, these were popular with the public, but they were not really creations. This type of work was uninspiring and would only have developed into a limited business venture, boring and sterile. After producing them in numbers to meet the demand – many destined for France – they stopped making them.

FIRST CREATIONS

One of the very first dolls that Lynne and Michael Roche created was Flora (1982), a lady doll on a kid body with, similar to the 19th century French lady dolls, upper wooden arms and lower bisque arms. Flora was not made in great quantities. Tiny Baby was also made in 1982. In 1983, the following year, they brought out Rosy.

Top, Flora and Tiny Baby
Bottom, Rosy Babies

16

For several years, simultaneously with their own original dolls, they were still producing a few replicas from their moulds of German babies, SFBJ characters, French and German bébés. These were completely phased out in the mid 1980s and the Roches then concentrated entirely on their own creations.

This leap into the unknown is a road paved with exacting demands and compelling obligations. In all domains, artists and creative people are always required to push their boundaries further and further. Difficult and demanding as it may be, Lynne and Michael Roche have not looked back since they set out on this path.

Around the same time, in the early 1980s, the French were developing their talents; the dolls of Anne Mitrani, Héloïse and Malou could be seen in the Ateliers d'Art, a professional salon held twice a year in Paris.

The German creators, innovators in Europe, had already started making dolls in the late 1970s and the names of Brigitte Deval, Sabine Esche and Annette Himstedt, not yet familiar, were just becoming known to those interested in this form of art, as well as influencing those beginning to make original dolls.

The American doll artists had been active from the 1960s onwards and the early group of precursors had enlarged and formed the National Institute of American Doll Artists (NIADA), of which Lynne and Michael are elected members.

It was also in the 1980s that attentive collectors were following the progress of creative doll making in the various countries and beginning to buy original dolls. Avant-garde, they inaugurated a new type of collection; that of contemporary dolls which were not just toys, but could be considered an art form.

Again Americans seem to be in the forefront. It is noteworthy that they, the collectors, and those far-sighted American specialized dealers who steadfastly promote American and European creation, like Danny and Barrie Shapiro of the Toy Shoppe, are instrumental in the greater development of a number of doll artists.

In 1973, Danny began to work with his father who had a toy distribution company – selling Fisher Price, Hasbro, Lego etc, and Sasha dolls – perhaps accounting for the natural evolution of Danny's taste in dolls. Leaving his father's business, Danny opened the Toy Shoppe in 1975, and started to attend the Nuremberg Toy Fair from 1978 onwards, seeking out fine toys and dolls. Danny met Barrie in the early 1980s, a key factor in the further progress of their business.

Not only have they, by their business acumen, been helping collectors to acquire dolls and bears, often though an accommodating system of payment, they have also been nurturing talent for some thirty years.

They can be compared to the late 19th early 20th century 'patron-buyer-dealers' of the Arts in Paris, supporting Vincent Van Gogh and Modigliani. Similarly, the Shapiros are visionary and intuitive, and have confidence in those they promote and in whom they believe.

They first began to sell Roche dolls in the early 1980s and became their main retailers in the States, before becoming their wholesalers and exclusive agents. This happened after the first catalogue promoting Hannah in 1988 and Claudine in 1989. And this continued until the creation of Ellie (2001), when they ceased being wholesalers generally. They continue to be their main retailers.

Danny Shapiro of the Toy Shoppe, Richmond U.S.A. says: *"I met Lynne and Michael very early in their career. At that time, I was seeking out finer and more well crafted dolls, and there were only a handful of artists making them at that time – late 1970s. Lynne and Michael were really in the fore-front of this modern doll movement that gained so much momentum by the mid 1980s. I immediately respected their dedication to fine hand craftsmanship, and loved the very personal and loving emotion that was put into their work. Their work has always reflected their own viewpoint, with no compromising to the commercial point of view. This quality only becomes better with age. On a personal note, Barrie and I can both say that Lynne and Michael have been true friends, and we value that relationship very much".*

In Great Britain, Tridias was one of the mainstays for many years. This toy company was expertly and intelligently run with much finesse by Charlotte and Robin Cooke – since retired from the profession, but still taking an active, personal interest in the Roche dolls. This company has slightly changed its initial orientation and no longer sells their dolls.

During Charlotte and Robin's reign (1966-1996), their toy shop sold a large array of toys carefully chosen for their design, craftsmanship and playability; and although the location in Bath did not promote artist dolls as such, you could find on the shelves of this progressive toy shop the dolls of Lynne and Michael Roche. The Cookes also promoted toys from the Toymakers Guild, of which the Roches are members – Lynne is on the committee.

Robin and Charlotte Cooke, former owners of Tridias in Great Britain say: *"We first got to know the Roches at an uniquely English event; a teddy bear convention, in the early 1980s at the Palace of Longleat, owned by the Marquis of Bath.*

Already Lynne had begun her progress of exquisitely designed dolls, with Michael an experienced furniture maker contributing brilliantly crafted wooden bodies.

We there began a warm personal relationship, and a business tie which lasted until we sold our small chain of toyshops fifteen years later. In the early days they did all their work on the premises of 'The China Doll', their shop in Bath, Michael in a workshop behind, knee deep in wood chips; Lynne at the counter, painting dolls faces and making clothes in a Dickensian environment, surrounded by shelf-loads of handmade miniatures, with a couple of cats on the counter. Lynne neatly solved the problems caused by the irritating intrusion of customers into this cosy environment by selling the shop to us.

They were a huge influence in our business; apart from introducing us to the rarefied world of collector dolls, and suggesting how to recognize the most distinguished, they helped us to create beautiful doll rooms and spaces in our shops, and took a dynamic interest for several years in the design and appearance of our mail order catalogues. We owe them a great deal."

The dedication of such enlightened people is an advantage, and advances doll creation as a whole. There are others – these are just two prime examples, on either side of the Atlantic.

"I think there is a very exciting level of doll making in Europe – people working in many mediums and with many interpretations of the 'doll' from near sculptures of great realism to stylized and mannered play dolls",

Lynne in the summer of 1989 in a conversation about creation.

A Lynne and Michael Roche doll is the fruit of a joint venture. Lynne and Michael each have their own area of expertise. They work together in total and admirable synergy. Simplifying the various steps without going into details, Lynne creates the heads, Michael the moulds, the porcelain hands and the bodies, (wood, porcelain, cloth) which are assembled. The heads are painted and wigged by Lynne and then she designs and creates the clothes.

Casting heads

But Michael, with his critical eye, intervenes and irons out problems even when it comes to the final modelling of the heads. His is the invisible touch, which is so important and complementary.

HEADS

Generally it takes some four months from the actual modelling of the head by Lynne to the final realization of the first doll in a finished stage, when it can be photographed.

But before sitting down to the modelling, signifying that the preparatory gestation is finished and the idea has taken on a more definite form, Lynne will have carried around, for some months, in her mind's eye, a vision,

intangible as yet, an idea that is developing, sparked off by an emotion from a fleeting view of a child, a photograph or a painting. Her art training makes her extremely perceptive to images, atmosphere and scenes.

She will sketch a few heads in her workbook to clarify and define more precisely the image that caught her fancy.

Like all creative work, the preliminary steps are invisible and much takes place when Lynne is involved in other daily activities. The difficult moment, as in writing, is when she has before her the 'white canvas' – here the painter in her is manifest – and she is obliged to make her vision materialize, become tangible, before developing it into the three-dimensional finished form of a doll.

Lynne's integrity is very much apparent in her attitude to her art. If, after modelling for some time, Lynne cannot 'feel' the head in preparation, and does not know where it is leading her, she destroys it. She must feel it and be at ease with it. Skill in modelling is not sufficient. Her sense of emotion must be present in it, for the doll to take on a life of its own. She says:

"A doll must have a core, I make it from the inside out. It is emotion that governs in creation. Quality and workmanship are not enough; the doll coming into being must first of all speak to me, before it can appeal to others."

Inspiration is just a small portion of the whole. It is the initial spark that ignites and fires the imagination, goading it to unsuspected depths of activity and creation.

Though the finished doll may seem artlessly simple – the true stamp of quality – it is, in fact, the outcome of intense creative work and a victory over inert forces.

Each doll is a challenge, each time renewed, to be carried through from the first steps of conception to the final realization. A daunting quest that Lynne puts herself through every year in order to create one or two new models, sometimes three.

From the clay head modelled by Lynne, Michael takes over. After critical modifications, he makes a plaster mould of it. From this, he then produces a master, and a cast which reproduces the heads. These are fired having gone through the various stages of preparation until they come back to Lynne who gives them their delicate colouring.

Top, master of Hannah and doll
Below, a modelled head
Right, back of finished head showing markings

Chatting about technical details, fascinated, I have watched Lynne in her studio, deftly wielding her fine paintbrushes at this task, whilst in the background the magic of Eric Satie's piano weaves another type of spell. The Roche dolls are composed of such sights and sounds for me. Another facet of their charm.

The heads return to a smaller kiln, where they are again fired to seal the colouring. The Roche dolls all have a diaphanous complexion; the porcelain of the head is delicately tinted, so like the finest of English skin colouring. This pale, translucent hue of the porcelain and the subtle colouring of their dolls' features remind me of some of the best French bébés, especially the early Bru dolls, or the E.J. Jumeau whose basic colouring is extremely pale.

Similar to a portrait in an oil painting or photograph, the head is the first thing that attracts the eye. It is through the features and the eyes that the soul is mirrored. This is where Lynne's art is evident. She excels in infusing the doll with a personality and presence of its own, unobtrusive but so very real.

Although a doll's primary appeal tends to be concentrated in its face, and however essential this may be, a doll is not just a head. It is also a body and clothing and ambience. The dolls of Lynne and Michael Roche always conform to this three-way rule. The resulting ensemble is their forte. This has been further developed with the years. Many more dolls are now created accompanied by tangible imaginative worlds, comprising of elaborate accessories; large-scale cars, big enough for a doll to sit in comfortably, space ships, doll's houses, theatres, Noah's Ark, ingenuous scenic backdrops which set the scene. This reflects how much care and thought Lynne invests in each doll, endowing it with background and a storyline which the collector may further embellish at will. The Roches are the precursors in this line of adding complete environments.

BODIES

All their dolls have carefully made, well proportioned bodies, wood or porcelain, and a more recent development, weighted covered jersey. In complete harmony with the whole; pleasing to look at, dressed and undressed. This is Michael's most direct, substantial contribution, another distinctive characteristic of the Roche dolls.

Michael's first attempt at a body in wood, entirely hand carved, conformed very much to a French body, only it was much heavier in form and weight. This body was destined for one of their reproductions in the early 1980s. The inspiration was an all-articulated lay figure, combined with Michael's natural ability to work in wood and construct things. Since this trial experiment, he has greatly improved upon the overall shape and experimented with various species of wood; now he uses lime exclusively. It is not too hard to carve, it has a general good even colour without too much grain, and it has the advantage of being fairly lightweight. Bodies are always a work in progress, as can be noted from the extensive series that Michael has developed during the last ten years.

Depending on the age they wish to portray, their dolls are assembled on a range of distinctive types of bodies. These are all composed of nine separate pieces not including the head and articulated with ball joints. In addition all the wooden bodies possess porcelain hands, with the exception of the large 'Early American Children' which have carved wooden hands.

The 23 inch dolls, like the large Sophy have a chunky toddler body with straight hip joints.

Those of 20 inches – large Hannah, Beth and Claudine are on a childlike form. The medium size of the above named models come on an identical but smaller version.

A toddler body with slanted hip joints and thick limbs is used for the 18 inch Florence, Freddy, Daisy and Sophy.

The smallest size dolls of all the models, measuring approximately 12 to 14 inches tall – Beth, Hannah, the four series II Early American Children, and Sophy are on an all porcelain, articulated, ball jointed body. This is an exact replica of the wooden one, in fact it is cast from a wooden body.

For the lady body of Anna (1992), the mother doll in the set with Polly, Michael was obliged to create a new type of body, with adult curves, more slender and elongated. He has also worked on the feet and is still trying to improve on them and make them more stylized.

Introduced in 1992, Polly – sold together with Anna as a special mother and child set – is a variation. Although she is 15 inches tall, she is mounted on a weighted cloth body, nicely covered with a flesh coloured jersey. Polly has bent porcelain arms.

The two sisters, Emily and Mary (1993), are on another differently shaped jointed body, more slender in form than any of the previous childrens' type bodies created by Michael. Then there are the babies such as Baby Tilly; these are generally found on cloth bodies with porcelain arms and legs. The Toddlers are miniature children, 4 inches high, and come on an all-porcelain, articulated body.

In 1996, Tansy and Gabrielle, two more adult-like dolls, with porcelain head and shoulder plate and porcelain limbs are to be found on a cloth body which has wooden joints at the shoulders enabling movement. This is a departure from the usual all-articulated, nine piece wooden body.

The Collectors Club dolls, Holly, Gigi and Lynne, are on all-bisque jointed bodies.

In 1997, Lillian is assembled on a body, long and slim and appropriate to her age group. The right scale is essential to the dolls overall appearance and Michael is ever vigilant.

In 1998, Michael worked on a new body type for Fleur and created a slender-bodied 17 inch doll.

Again, in 2001, he designed a new child's wooden articulated body used for Ellie and Louisa. That same year, Molly baby also had a newly constructed soft body.

From 1997 onwards, the soft bodies have been designed by Sue Ralph. Sue, as a diversion to her own work as well as enjoying the challenge of adding art to a body form in cloth, has also designed and created new innovative articulated bodies in cloth for the Roche dolls from Tabitha (1998) onwards and Maggie (2003).

From the above, it is easy to discern that Michael is forever trying out new techniques, inventing appropriate body designs, improving feet and body forms. He is very successful in his area of expertise. The reason for the overall excellence of their dolls is the careful workmanship that goes into their creation. It is a continuous ongoing process. The body is an important component of a doll. All the Roche dolls are easily poseable; they can stand nicely erect without the help of a doll stand, and are stable. With their system of articulation and joints they can adapt to all situations, and if they were not collector's items, they could be a wonderful child's plaything because of their inherent quality of playability. They are easy to manipulate, dress and undress, which is an added attraction for some collectors.

I was pleased and in complete agreement with Lynne's opinion when she told me: *"A doll should articulate, in fact I love the designs of bodies of dolls. I always enjoy undressing old dolls and looking at them in the 'nude'. I feel they should look good in that state also."* The Roche dolls certainly do look good in that state.

CLOTHES

A doll can be ruined and made insignificant by
inappropriate dress. Its personality is strengthened and its
appeal enhanced and reinforced by relevant clothes.
Clothing is an important factor and here the quintessential
quality of Englishness of the Roche dolls is at its peak.
From Lynne's sketchbook the nascent doll comes into
being, developing its allure and style through its dress.
A delight to thumb through, these sketchbooks are
precious and neat like the dolls themselves. Together with
ideas and drawings there is a colourful selection of samples
of material, appropriately scaled if they happen to be
patterned, and luminous variegated strands of soft wools.

Lynne's flair for creating extremely pleasant
combinations of colour schemes and marrying textures
like printed cottons and hand-knitted garments is another
distinctive stamp, and identifies their dolls as surely as a
signature. Much care and attention to detail is given to the
outfit of each new doll; like tiny buttons, a handy pocket in
which to place a small toy, a brooch, an amusing animal
inlay on the back of a knitted jumper; or appliqués,
quaintly decorating the bottom of a cotton pinafore, or
offsetting the front of the bodice like the dutch doll and
the golly.

The Roche dolls are not dressed in any particular fashion
and their appeal is timeless. Their clothes do not follow a
mode, they are neither in fashion nor out of fashion, they
do not cultivate nostalgia and are definitely not of the
romantic trend. Lynne says with a smile. *"They are nearly
contemporary."* The painter in Lynne sees a whole. Her
creations are the fruit of discriminating taste and gifted
resourceful talent.

23

In 1982, working from the shop premises, 'The China Doll', they produced their first original dolls – Rosy, Flora and Tiny Baby.

Starting from 1984, all dolls are marked with the year of copyright. They are signed by Lynne behind the doll's left ear – marked LGR and the two last digits of the year e.g 01 for 2001.

Future reference for dating purposes; the dolls, dated by the year of their copyright incised on the neck, are in reality not to be found on the market that same year.

They are on sale from the next year onwards. For example, Lillian was created in 1996, she is marked 1996 but she appears in the 1997 catalogue and is new for 1997. All the dates cited in the text are those from the catalogue, i.e the year that the dolls were on sale.

Each year, some older models are phased out and replaced by two or three new creations, as well as several special limited editions.

The new dolls are available at the beginning of the following year, in time for the Toy Fairs; British Toy Makers Guild, Nuremberg and New York.

For fourteen years, from 1985, they journeyed backwards and forwards over the Atlantic and between Germany and Bath, attending these Professional Toy Fairs, starting with New York Toy Fair in 1985, then the prestigious Nuremberg Toy Fair in 1987. Since 1999, they have not travelled abroad to these annual Toy Fairs, except in 2001 when they returned to New York, preferring to concentrate and devote their time to the dolls. Travelling has not been as necessary because direct contact can be maintained with shops using email and the web, and with collectors by attending NIADA, UFDC, and their own Open Day.

At Doll Art
Left – right, Monika, Stephanie Blythe, a member of press, Malou, Joelle (Heloise dolls) Karin Schmidt, Lynne, Anne Mitrani and Edna Daly

For several years running, in the early 1990s the Roches were present, with a peer group of fellow doll artists, at Doll Art, a specialized exhibition held in Frankfurt, Germany.

In the autumn of 1995, the year when Simon and Katy appeared, they had a show in Gillian Still's Gallery in Llandeilo, Wales.

At Llandeilo

INSPIRATION

The Roche dolls are not realistic portraits in the manner of the German artists. Although she admires the meticulous originals of Sabine Esche, Lynne does not

Top, Michael at Nuremburg
Below, at Nuremburg Toy Fair
Bottom, at New York Toy Fair
Right – left, Michael, Danny Shapiro, Barrie Shapiro and Lynne

reproduce in this fashion the features of her dolls. She can however be inspired and influenced by a fleeting vision of a child she has seen outdoors, like the wispy blond haired little girl weighed down with a huge teddy which translated into the charming Sophy (1991). A medium sized Sophy is another of the Roches dolls in the Decorative Arts collection). Old photographs, illustrations in magazines, paintings, are all food for her inspiration. It is the general ambience, the total look that fires her imagination. Her dolls are neither characters nor direct portraits but personal definitions and an interpretative vision.

Colettes

For example, Colette (1982) was one of their earliest dolls and came in three sizes. She was a free personal representation of a photograph of the French writer Colette as a child, a favourite author of Lynne's – who is an avid reader. As with all their dolls, the smallest size Colette (13 inches), is on the all-porcelain body, articulated with wooden joints. This small Colette was remarked upon and chosen by the organizers of *Save the Children Fund* to be dressed by thirty-five British couturiers for exhibition, and afterwards a charity sale held at Sothebys. Some of the top fashion designers including Hardy Amies, Laura Ashley, John Bates, Bruce Oldfield, Zandra Rhodes, Michael Fish and Mary Quant costumed and hairstyled their Colettes variously. The dolls were then displayed in the stately home of Longleat House in Wiltshire before the auction in 1984. These dolls are invested with a double attraction for collectors.

From here on, the year given is that when the doll was available on the market for collectors to buy.

Florence (1985), muffled up in her duffle coat, woollen

Florence and Freddy

bonnet, scarf and sheep skin lined boots, was inspired by the image of an English child dressed in many layers of clothing to guard against the cold of winter. It was through the photograph of a charming winter scene depicting Florence and Freddy that I first noticed and appreciated the Roche dolls. Here the gentle appeal of their personalities shines out of the tiny illustration. Freddy, together with Claudine (1989), are part of the collection of artist dolls in the Decorative Arts Museum in Paris, and they figured in the Exhibition 'Poupées de Hier, Créations d' Aujourd'hui' in 1992.

Daisy (1986) is an imaginative interpretation of a sturdy child of school age, firmly planted on her two feet, tummy forward, ready to scowl at you at the least occasion. She is not pretty and dainty, she is awkward but she has real character. Small Daisy, clad in her red corduroy dungarees, alias 'Plum Pudding', as she was affectionately nicknamed by Antoinette de Rohan and myself when we were setting up the summer exhibition in the museum of Josselin (France) in 1988, is known to us by this name alone, when we speak of her now. As I

Daisy

have 'played' with her and handled her whilst arranging the display, she occupies a special fond place in my memory, even if in Lynne's own words *"she didn't quite work out!"*

Alice (1987) was transposed from the 19th century photographs of Alice Liddell, the little girl who gave her name to Lewis Caroll's book 'Alice in Wonderland'. Some years later, Lynne will be again inspired by the original illustrations by Tennial, and Jessica (2000), was dressed as Alice from his drawings.

Already, through the above dolls and those that will follow, one becomes aware of the importance attached to a doll's name. Like costume, it is a special part of the doll. Few of the Roche dolls are misnamed. Each is at ease with its name. Curious, I questioned Lynne how she names their dolls. She replied that she is influenced by the painters, authors and the people she admires most.

Early American Children series II

The first of the series Early American Children (1989) is a limited edition of 30. The two large 28 inch size dolls and the four smaller, more recent, 12 inch ones (1991) were all inspired by, but not copied from, early 19th century primitive American paintings of children with their toys. Again the keen perception of the painter in Lynne is at work and influences her.

Similar to these 19th century painted portraits, Elizabeth and Jacob and the later, series II Early American

Children (1991) are accompanied by specially handmade carved wooden toys – accessories being another distinguishing feature of their dolls.

Hannah (introduced in 1988 but created in 1987) was a breakthrough in the Roches ever growing popularity. The innovation is Hannah's features. There is more vigour, definition and harmony in the modelling, revealing a presence, and a personality that is more achieved and stronger. This seems to be a turning point in their creative work, when art takes over from good craftsmanship.

1987 was the year in which their lifestyle of work was modified. The shop 'The China Doll' was taking up a greater part of Lynne's time, leaving her too little freedom to continue to create. They sold the shop and acquired a house in Lansdown.

Beth and baby Tilly

Beth with Baby (1990), were the first dolls bought by Antoinette de Rohan for the Musée de Poupées in Josselin (Morbihan, France).

Antionette de Rohan says: *"Since the Musée de Poupées in Josselin opened in 1984, in which our family collection of dolls and toys is on display, I have exhibited, on numerous occasions, dolls created by Lynne and Michael Roche. In fact, since the first temporary exhibition on 'Doll creation, Past and Present' which took place in 1989, (which included Daisy) there has rarely been a year when they are not present in the museum.*

I derive great pleasure in setting them up in the showcases, like this year, Jessica (2000) as Red Riding Hood who fits in beautifully with the current 2004 summer exhibition inspired by literature, fairy tales, film and comic strip characters.

Visitors to the museum always express admiration of the Roche dolls, they especially appreciate the gentle serenity of their features and the refined outfits realized with such good taste, ingenuity and inventive skill.

The Rohan collection is proud to have in its inventory a number of the creations of Lynne and Michael Roche."

The work of the American painter Mary Cassatt whom Lynne greatly admires, was the source of inspiration for the creation of Anna and Polly, mother and child in 1992.

Akin to Cassatt's painting of motherhood, where mother and offspring are portrayed, as Lynne says, *"Without sentimentality, bound for time immemorial in an intimate scene of their daily relationship."* These two dolls, Anna and Polly, relate to one another harmoniously. Polly with her soft weighted cloth body blends in beautifully to her elegant mother, Anna.

Lynne and cousin Gill

Lynne is particularly interested in developing interrelation between dolls and the 1993 edition was created with this goal specifically in mind. Emily and Mary (1993) are two sisters who have a special relationship together. This time the starting point of Lynne's imagination was a batch of old photographs, in fact Lynne's own family snaps.

1994 is a vintage year, fruitful with three new models, all very different. With these another plateau has been attained. It is also in this year that the Roches made major changes in their production. They decided no longer to make dolls with all-porcelain bodies, with the exception of one little baby, in order to concentrate essentially on the larger dolls and offer more accessories and clothing. Part of this year's promotion is a large-scale wooden chest of drawers with various accessories, a carry cot, a metal clothes stand complete with wooden hangers and various outfits for 20/21 inch dolls.

A photograph of a little Chinese girl, round moon-shaped face wearing a serious expression, attracted Lynne's eye and inspired her to create Sam and his sister, Violet. These two 21 inch dolls with Asian features come on a nine piece wooden body with porcelain hands.

Henrietta (1994) was also new for this same year, and was available in two editions. I have a particularly soft spot for the blue-eyed, frizzy blond haired Henrietta, very striking in her red duffle coat, denim dungarees, scarf, and mittens, holding a classic fully jointed bear by the Welsh maker, Bocs Teganau. The pensive look of a small child is successfully captured and tangibly translated into an appealing three dimensional doll. Baby Lily and Baby Amy, two 7 inch babies – one with an Asian look – are the third of the new models; they have porcelain heads, painted eyes, and porcelain limbs mounted on a cloth torso filled with pellets for poseability.

Three new models came out in 1995 – Simon, a 23 inch boy doll characterizing a real boy and Katy, who was inspired by a visit to Wales and the children seen playing on the beaches there, collecting shells.

Lynne, who has a great love of the old 19th century wax babies and dolls, tried her hand again in wax and created Juliet, who has a sculpted wax head, shoulders, arms and legs on a cloth body. Her source was a painting by John Wilson Waterhouse (1849-1917), a Victorian artist. The 1995 catalogue also includes an appealing series of 7 inch babies looking mischievous in their whimsical animal outfits created by Lynne in fine angora wools. They have porcelain heads with painted eyes and are on a weighted soft body.

New creations for 1996 are Susannah, 20 inch, portraying an older child and Lizzie, 13 inches, who could represent a younger sister, who interrelate nicely. Again Lynne has captured a wistful childlike innocence with Lizzie.

Departing from the usual jointed all-articulated wooden bodies to be found on the majority of the Roche dolls, Tansy and Gabrielle, new for this year, have a fitted shoulder plate, assembled on a cloth body with porcelain arms and legs and wood joints at the shoulder. These two dolls have more mature countenances.

In 1997 Lynne created Lillian, who has pensive elfin pointed features, gamine like, and an innovative, more mature, facial expression. She is on a special slender body made by Michael, who determines the scale and shape of the body in accordance with the age the doll represents. Lillian's face was a source of inspiration for the style of clothing that Lynne designed for her. Heidi, a smaller 13 inch doll accompanied by her own special papier mâché Japanese doll, is new for this year. And a third completely different type of doll for 1997 is Baby Pip, 10 inch, with porcelain arms and legs mounted on a cloth body.

The Collectors Club came into being in May 1997. Holly is the first club doll, articulated and all-porcelain. However, it is not every year that a new doll is created for the Club members; sometimes it can be accessories, like a trunk complete with specially made outfits.

Both the dolls created for 1998 are on completely different types of body; Michael's most direct contribution. Fleur is on a new slim body allowing extra movement, designed and carved by Michael, with slender carved feet and porcelain hands. She can have either inset glass or painted eyes. It is amazing how her facial expression can be changed with these different interpretations of her eyes.

Tabitha, who is 20 inches, has more childlike features. She is on a sturdy, but very poseable, soft cloth body with porcelain hands.

Laura, May Rose and Thomas are three contrasting models brought out in 1999. Laura is 17 inches tall on an all-articulated carved limewood body with porcelain hands. On this occasion, Lynne's source of inspiration was a photograph of a round-faced contemplative child. Her personality is subtly outlined through the three different outfits designed for her by Lynne. Evidence of Lynne's versatile talent appears when an identical doll can appear to be so different depending on the clothes she is wearing. May Rose is distinguished by delicate Japanese type features, 20 inches tall on a slender hand-carved articulated limewood body, dressed in a kimono style outfit or an ensemble reminiscent of the orient. The little toddler boy, Thomas, could be Tabitha's young playmate.

Estelle Johnston from Atlanta U.S.A. says: *"Dolls, by their very nature, are stylized representations rather than realistic portrayals of the human species. Until the 19th century dolls were highly stylized and, as the quantity of production increased toward the middle of the century, only rarely did they resemble an actual individual human face or attain the status of a portrait doll. With the emergence of doll makers concentrating on the child in the 20th century this began to change and the creations of artists like Käthe Kruse and Dewees Cochran reflected real children. Perhaps it was this influence which has led to a virtual explosion of artists producing life-like child dolls today. The work of a few really caught my eye, beginning with Lynne and Michael Roche. Lynne manages to skilfully tread the fine line between the past and the present. Her delicacy of touch in the sculpting, her realistically sized and expressively set dolls' eyes, her taste in the quality of bisque, in wigs, in hand-dyed and handmade clothing with a definite retrospective flavour – all bespeak her love of antique dolls. Yet her children are also of today and somehow very human. It has not been the least bit difficult for this long time collector of antique dolls to also become a devotee and student of Lynne and Michael Roche's work and of their development as creators of magical children."*

The Roches 20th anniversary in 2000 is marked by a special collection with The World of Storybooks, starring a cast of four new creations: Jessica, Stephen, Michael and friends, who become Red Riding Hood, Alice and Hansel and Gretel. This is a new venture into the realm of story-book character dolls, influenced by the work of the Austrian illustrator of children's books, Lizbeth Zwerger, for whom Lynne has great admiration. Chloe is Thomas's (1999) new sister, on a similar cloth body and they play Jack and Jill together.

Three new models are in the 2001 catalogue, Ellie, Louisa and new Molly Baby. Lynne was stirred by a painting by German Academic Johan Georg Meyer von Bremen (1813-1886) of two children bending over, looking at a baby in a cot. Ellie's expression was inspired by that of the younger child. Again Michael has been at work creating new bodies with childlike proportions for Ellie and Louisa. New Molly Baby is a large 15 inch baby on a slightly weighted newly designed cloth body with porcelain hands. Available in traditional knitted outfits or continuing the story book theme, she stars as Rock-a-Bye-Baby in a felt nest, complete with blue bird.

2002 is a year of innovation with a small size 11 inch doll, Kitty. This is the first time the Roches have designed such a small doll, on an all-articulated wooden body with porcelain hands – a challenge that Michael rose to, in creating a body on such a small a scale. Although Kitty is the only new creation for this year, much thought has surrounded her and she is developed with four different settings, one for each season.

Two more small 11 inch size dolls, Dorothy and Emile, join Kitty in 2003. They are accompanied by large in-scale toys and accessories such as a doll's house, bed, car and space ship into which Emile fits snugly.

Full round-face Maggie is a large 20 inch creation for 2003. She is on a newly developed cloth body with joints at the elbows and knees and a system at the neck allowing her extra movement for expressive posing.

In 2004, Flossie is the fourth small doll of the series inaugurated by Kitty in 2002. Likewise she is 11 inches tall, on an articulated limewood body with porcelain hands, and similar to the three preceding her, she comes with a variety of backdrops and in-scale toys.

Nan is a new soft bodied, older type doll than Maggie (2003), from whom she was developed. She is 18 inches on a more shapely mature body with additional articulation. Nan, as the French Provencal girl, is most attractive in her warm hued, colourful provincial type ensemble.

It was also in 2004 that Lynne made a special edition of ten dolls for Teddy Bears of Witney representing Princess Xenia, inspired by a photograph of the young Princess who is holding Alfonso, a Steiff bear. Ian Pout, the owner of Teddy Bears of Witney, bought the unique original 1908 red mohair bear in its cotton sateen Cossack tunic, accompanied by its moving tragic story, at a record breaking Christie's auction in 1989. The Steiff firm, a year later, reproduced a limited edition of this historic bear specially for Ian Pout, and several years later a smaller Baby Alfonso.

Doll of Princess Xenia

2005 is a jubilee year, a landmark, celebrating Lynne and Michael Roches 25th anniversary of doll making. Adding to the growing family of small dolls (Kitty, Dorothy, Emile) are three new creations with Mimi, 10.5 inch, Annie, 12 inch and baby Pom Pom, 8 inch.

These new members of the 'small clan' all have special toys, a wooden locomotive, a double seater swinging fairground gondola and their own quirky dogs.

For this special anniversary year, Lynne has written, illustrated and handmade a small limited edition book telling the story of Annie Rosemary Browning. The doll, Annie Rosemary, comes with a handmade trunk decorated with illustrations by Lynne, a small doll, a silver Annie brooch and a beautiful workbox which includes tiny silver scissors, needle case, buttons…and of course, her little brown cat. This is a very select limited edition.

Lynne has been very active these past two years writing children's stories which she also illustrates. 'The Happiest Christmas' is being published by Reverie (U.S.A.) in 2005. The stories that she has spun around her dolls over the years, endowing them with a consistency, and depth, personalizing them, have come full circle with the forthcoming publication, as well as the edition of 'Annie Rosemary Browning'. They have materialized from one aspect of her creative invention – the dolls, and taken flight and further developed into something tangible born from her artistic talents and her love of books.

THE COLLECTORS CLUB

The Collectors club is a recent innovation which grew out of Lynne's wish for more direct contact with collectors, especially her English followers. Some hundreds have joined, originating from Greece, Luxembourg, Germany, Holland, Japan, France and the United States. And the list is increasing.

Lynne inaugurated the Collectors Club in May 1997. Members receive an annual newsletter in colour, which includes the details of the Fairs where their dolls will be present. Collectors can consult an up-to-date website, created in 2000, www.roche-dolls.co.uk. For the Club, Lynne proposes each year various limited unique editions, outfits and accessories, made exclusively for the members, who are also invited to the Open Day, on the second Saturday in December.

The Roches Open Day is an event not to be missed, a pleasant prelude to the festive season of Christmas, when some 40 staunch collectors from near and far – Scotland, Wales, France, Holland, the United States – gather together to spend several extremely pleasant hours. Two other English artists, Jill Bennett, with her historically precise, much in demand, costumed doll's house doll's, and Jane Davies with her appealing miniature children, also participate in the event.

Dillies

Lynne with scooter

Almost all of the Roches dolls are distinguished by the special accessories, detailed clothing, real jewellery, and expertly made toys that accompany them. Lynne takes particular care to ensure that each Sophy, like the real little girl who caught her eye, is carrying an attractive mohair teddy bear, a collector's item in itself, made by the American company Bearly There. For later dolls Violet and Sam, Lynne chose the bears from the Welsh company Bocs Teganau.

A wonderful plush and felt elephant, Tabitha's toy pet, comes from the German company Kozen, who make finely modelled plush animals.

For several years now many of the Roches creations have been accompanied by neat, handmade painted wooden toys, specially designed for them by craftsmen, artists or specialized miniaturists.

The wooden toys of the Early American Children second series were designed by Tim Rossiter. At that time he was making dollhouse miniatures but, approached by Lynne, he worked in a larger scale. A fine artist, Rossiter has further developed his talents in this domain and he has designed and created many special feature pieces for the Roche

Heidi and her toy box

dolls: the dollhouse, an Ark which is a collector's item in itself, the open cars and the spaceship.

The tiny wooden amazingly fully-jointed 'Dutch dolls' found in Claudine's pocket and decorating Ellie's bodice come from Eric Horne, a well-known name in modern wooden toys who also makes wonderful gollys and other items inspired by the books of Florence K. Upton.

Accompanying some of the earlier dolls, like Hannah, the Lilliputian doll brooches and the dolls teddies were invented by the nimble fingers of Gillian Heal.

Carolyn Brewer is an 'ace knitter' – Lynne's own words – who copies and interprets Lynne's original knit wear designs. She is the inventor of the wonderful, whimsical knitted cats and dogs that are part of the story of many of the more recent dolls.

Ann Flint has for ten years, as an outworker, faithfully made from Lynne's designs the tiny superb handmade clothing that dress so many Roche models.

A well-known Bath jeweller, Nicholas Wylde, devised the tiny jewellery, for example Anna's earrings, using real stones. When Lynne approached him with this request, he was amused but not averse to trying his hand in miniature. The special sister sets have unique silver charm bracelets created by him.

The Collectors Club silver enamelled pin, offered to each new subscriber, is designed by him. In the 2005 edition, Lynne has added a pair of his exquisite miniature silver scissors, together with other accessories, as part of a tiny sewing box, a jewel in itself created by Janette Sawyer, who used to work at a couture house in London.

In these later years Sue Williams, Lynne's cousin, has been doing some needlework, reproducing from Lynne's original costumes, carefully sewn outfits. I see the pleasure and satisfaction mirrored in her face when she brings back her finished work. Many years ago Sue, aged 15 or so, gave a very young Lynne a present of a small doll dressed in knitted clothes that she had made especially for it. The wheel has come full circle. Destiny?

Sue Ralph, who previously had her own clothing business in South Africa, is now a Bath resident and once worked at the Bath Costume museum. She has fashioned some of the historically correct period ensembles like the Jane Austen piece with a trunk.

For Lynne this is an unusual occurrence because she derives great pleasure in creating each costume, each outfit; inventing, neither copying nor reproducing. Choosing the different materials, having them dyed to her specifications with natural dyes, matching the colours, selecting the tiny buttons, inventing knitwear that even the top fashion designers would not disclaim, or doing the appliqué work herself, are all part of the creative impulse that each doll requires to make it an entity. Each is endowed with its own specific personality.

Lynne, like all inspired doll makers, ever seeking exciting new resources, titbits and materials, always has her eyes and mind tuned to her craft, forever looking for things that will work or send her off in a new direction. And, wherever she goes she is constantly searching for special little accessories, or for people liable to be interested in creating new playthings, or supply her with the very best of materials. Nothing is too fine or too much trouble to research and find.

All these small details are precious and add to the overall refinement of their dolls.

Emile with Spaceship

In 1988, outgrowing the possibilities of limited workspace in the shop in Walcot Street, the Roches bought a high, narrow 18th century house on Lansdown Hill where they combine their living and working quarters. In view of their increasing success, it was obvious that they needed to enlarge their work-site in order to accommodate the further development of their activity.

They sold the shop, 'The China Doll' to Robin and Charlotte Cooke, owners of the Tridias toyshops. With the new location, Lansdown, and its possibilities of space, they were able to rationalize and render the task of living and working easier, although the fact that they do both in the same premises makes the division more difficult, and in all probability they work harder and longer hours. It is always tempting to return to your studio if you only have to walk across a corridor to get there.

Is there any correlation between the more visible achievement of their dolls from 1987 onwards and this radical change of working conditions? Was Lansdown the catalyst? Or was it just due to the normal sequence of their evolution? Whatever the reason, it is from this epoch that this 'quality plus' and harmony is visible, and it grows stronger in each new creation. Claudine, Beth, Sophy, Anna all conform to this consolidation of their talents. Anna and the 1993 sisters are most vibrant examples. Elegant Lillian and May Rose are yet another superb facet of the Roches professional accomplishment. With their delicate refined features, they represent a more adult aspect, a domain that they had not previously much visited.

Here in Lansdown, from the basement – Michael's domain – to the highest of the five floors, they have established various workrooms, ateliers, living quarters, bedrooms etc. All this blends in, sometimes overlapping, like Lynne's own studio, which adjoins the sitting room.

It is from this small room, on the second floor, overlooking the long, narrow garden, a terrestrial replica of the tall house, that Lynne works and reflects in the congenial company of one, two or three of

the cats, who sit or lie on the end of her table on a cushion, mulling over delicate thoughts as the clouds blow by. Why not all six of them? Because you will be sure to find Sam, Emily or Flossie watchful over Michael in the basement as he is sanding bodies or achieving some stage of work in porcelain.

On two sides of the room, shelves climb to the ceiling; one wall filled, spilling over with books; doll books, books on art, on childhood; the other, a dressmaker's delight: containing skeins and bobbins of wonderful hued wools, tiny drawers of buttons, dolls eyes, fragile specially made tiny jewellery, neat tagged boxes of colourful wools. Then there are the trays of heads perched on any available surface, waiting for the eye spaces to be cut out by Lynne, or heads smoothed and painted. Several of Lynne's treasured antique dolls benevolently watch over the daily activities. Who they are? Of course; a Käthe Kruse model number 1, two early, slightly worn Steiff little boy and girl, and an American Kamkins are amongst the most prized of the 20th century dolls. As well as several beautiful 19th century French bébés, manufactured by Jumeau and Bru.

About eight years ago she also started collecting stuffed animals and bears, favouring Steiff of course. But the contemporary bear creation scene has also caught her eye. And the work of several American artists and companies, fanciful and full of wit are perched on shelves or sit on the computer, overseeing Lynne while she is at work.

In this comfortable atmosphere, ideas are tried and rejected, the sketchbook consulted, heads are modelled, the doll takes on a life of its own, and faces spring to life from the palette under Lynne's competent paint brush. Emails and faxes are sent and received. Long overseas conversations are held on the telephone, CDs are played: Lynne's days are always accompanied and coloured by music.

In all, at the present time they are able to produce approximately two hundred dolls annually – composed of one or two new creations and special limited series, as well as the continuing production of four or five models in their two or three sizes.

The Roche dolls from 1986/87, and especially those dating from the early 1990s onwards, possess an inherent personal quality and an unmistakable presence.

The 21st century creations, Jessica, Kitty, Emile, Nan, confirm the continuation and reinforcement of their art.

They epitomize a quintessential Englishness, comprehensible and eloquent.

Their neatly finished dolls do not bow to nostalgia, although the initial form of the bodies may resemble that of the 19th century bébés. The Roches are not influenced by transitory modes, complying with the whims of fashion or tendencies of the present, interpreting public taste. Their dolls retain a distinctive, specific character, often poignant, unique to the Roches alone.

The natural simplicity of the dolls contains a power of appeal which moves and tugs at the emotions in some way or other. This 'artlessness' provokes a feeling of tenderness as well as developing a sense of complicity.

A Roche doll shines with an interior light and glows with serenity. It is infused with a gentle charisma of its own, it is never intruding, nor aggressively attractive. It has warmth, charm and personality.

A craftsman shows skill in technical details. An artist shows imagination. The Roches combine the two.

Their dolls are very much a part of the history of creative doll making at the end of the 20th and the beginning of the 21st century. Their place in posterity is assured.

This edition, celebrating the 25th anniversary of their doll creation, confirms that this longevity is the consequence of continued reflection, professional integrity and an everyday involvement in, and dedication to the difficult world of creation.

It is a worthy homage to their work and pays a merited tribute to their art form.

GALLERY

In the Gallery section, we have arranged pictures of the original dolls we have made over the last 25 years in some of their editions. We hope you enjoy this retrospective of our work.

Lynne Roche

Michael Roche

Colette (1982). 20", all wooden
body. Numbered edition.

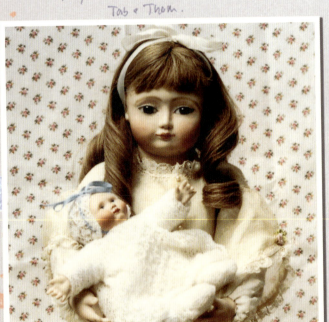

Flora (1982), 20", bisque head, arms and shoulderplate, with a leather body. Tiny baby 6", on a cloth body, with bisque head and hands.

Colette (1982), 18" and 20", with wooden bodies. Colette 13" on an all bisque body.

40

Daisy, 18", wood body.

Florence (1984), Daisy (1985) and
Florence, 18", on wooden bodies.

Florence, 18".

Freddy, 18", Florence, 18" and Alice
(1986), 20", all on wooden bodies.

43

Alice and her trunk, limited edition 20".

Small Alice, 15", all bisque body.

Minet Cherie (1985), 6", porcelain head, hands and
lower legs and with her leather trunk and accessories.

Amy, Lucy, Tom and Tim, (1986), 4.5", all bisque toddlers.

1) ryelin + coat e hat   pink/apricot
   dress   (wool from N·Sh?)...
                                    ...t blu...
                                    ...aten
                                    any
                                    gree
                                    Pi...

Wax baby, 5".

...s love one so much—more than they will allow But they have so
...h wisdom they keep it to themselves

46

Poppy (1989), 22", and Beth (1989),
20", on wooden bodies, with Chui, Lynne
and Michael's first cat, in their garden.

Claudine (1988), 20", Beth and Hannah (1987), on wooden bodies.

1. Two Claudines, 20", with Beth, 20".

2. Claudine and Hannah, 20".

3. Beth, Claudine and Hannah, 18".

Hannah, 20" and 18", wooden bodies, with small Hannah, 15", on an all-bisque body.

'Christmas Shopping' Claudine, 20" and
Georgy, 18", with baby, on a cloth body.
A Christmas edition for the Toy Shoppe.

10th anniversary Beth, 15",
on an all-bisque body.

Claudine, Hannah and Beth, 15".

New Baby (1987), 10", with bisque arms and legs, on a cloth body, with 2 Tilly babies.

Hannah, 20", with New Baby.

Sophy (1990), 22", with a wooden body.

Sophy, 18", with
wooden body.

Poppy (1989), 22", and
Sophies, all with wooden body.

Handwritten annotations (upper margin):

1) V.yellll + coat e hat pink/apricot dress
2) ___ ___ (wool from N.Sh?) ___
3) other dress with knitted wool blues coat e hat
___ ___ printed material

___ dress w angora bows?
pink.
___ mice, hates
___ beings
— Oliver Herford

All-bisque Emily and Mary, 15" and 16".

Special one-of-a-kind sisters, Mary and Emily (1992), 18" and 19", on wooden bodies. Produced for the Toy Fair New York.

Special one-of-a-kind sisters Mary and Emily, 18" and 19", on wooden bodies. Produced for Toy Fair New York.

Early American Children II
(1990), 12", all bisque bodies.

Large Early American Children, Elizabeth and
Jacob (1989), 28", all wooden bodies and hands.

Wax Juliet (1994), 18", wax arms,
legs and head, with a cloth body.

55

Anna (1991), 21", on a wooden body, and Polly
(1991), 12", with bisque head and arms, cloth body.

Special one-of-a-kind Anna and
Polly for Toy Fair New York.

Billy, 18", who loves
cricket, on a wooden body.

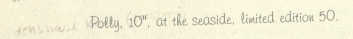
Polly, 10", at the seaside, limited edition 50.

58

Henrietta (1993), 21", Violet and Sam
(1993), 21", all on wooden bodies.

Violet and Sam, 20",
both on wooden bodies.

Henrietta, 20".

Baby Lily and Baby Amy (1993), 6", on
bisque head, arms and legs, with a cloth body.

15th anniversary Katy (1994), 18", on a wooden body, with tiny Florence, limited edition 50.

At dinner time he would sit in a corner, concentrating, and suddenly they would say, "Time to feed the cat," as if it were their own idea.

Lilian Jackson Braun

63

Simon (1994), 23" and Katy, 20", on wooden bodies.

Katy, 20".

Susannah (1995), 20",
on a wooden body.

Knitted
Kimono

Gigi outfit
Tabitkas outfits   } Janette.
  „ red suit   ?
  new dress   Ann?

Susannah with Lizzie (1995), 15", both with wooden bodies.

At dinner time he would sit in a corner, concentrating,
and suddenly they would say, "Time to feed the cat,"
as if it were their own idea.

Lilian Jackson Braun

67

Lillian (1996) and Susannah, 20", showing the clothing that is available separately.

Lizzies, 15".

A kitten is chiefly remarkable for rushing about like mad at nothing whatever, and generally stopping before it gets there.

Agnes Repplier

Tansy and Gabrielle (1995), 20",
bisque head, shoulder plate, arms
and legs, with a cloth body.

69

Lillian, 20".

Lillians (1996).
on wooden bodies.

71

Punch and Judy Lizzies, Baby Pips
(1996) and Martha (1997).

NEXT
SHOW
3:00 PM

Two Heidis (1996), 15", all on wood bodies, with Japanese dolls of papier mâché.

Lizzie and Pip go boating, one-of-a-kind for Musée de la Poupée, Paris (1996).

Baby Pip.

75

Fleur (1997), 18", at the ballet, limited edition 30.

Fleur on a wood body.

Fleur.

May Rose (1998), 20".

May Rose (1998), 20".

Tabitha (1997), 20" and Thomas
(1998), 18", on cloth bodies.

Laura (1998), 18", wooden body.

Laura with doll's house,
limited edition 5.

Lauras, with wooden bodies.

82

Owl and Pussy-Cat, Jessica (1999), as Pussy-Cat, 19", with Michael (1999) as Owl, 18", with wooden bodies, limited edition 25.

habutai bodice
dyed photo logwood
little ribbon

Jessica as Alice in Wonderland, and
Little Red Riding-hood, limited edition 50.

Jessica and Stephen 19", as Hansel
and Gretel, limited edition 25.

Stephen, Jessica
and Michael.

Chloe (1999), as Goldilocks,
limited edition 20.

Chloe and Thomas.

Baby Molly (2000), 12",
bisque head and hands, on a cloth body
Hush-a-bye-baby, limited edition 20.

Ellie, 19", on a
wooden body.

Louisa and Ellie (2000).

Louisa and Ellie.

Kitty Winter (2001), 11.5", on a wooden body.

Little Red Ridinghood

Hansel & Gretle

Goldilocks?

Cindrella

A...

3

2

4

2 x

cool net Laura's
C   middle nest/Laura
    1 & 2
T
    3 & 4
Thomas & Tab
    5 & 6
    Japanese
Back Very c/v or 2 Laura or
        Tab & Thom.

Kitty (2001), with boat and car, limited edition 35 and 25.

100

155.50.

165.00

Dorothy (2002) and Emile (2002), 11.5", with car, all with wooden bodies, limited edition 25. With doll's house, limited edition 35. Emile with spaceship, limited edition 10.

"Little Red Ridinghood"

Goldilocks?

Cinderella

Alice

90

Emile with spaceship, limited edition 10. Winter Dorothy, limited edition 50.

91

1) car - gosford park

2) dolls house knit dress - mohair

3) winter w tree

4)

Dorothy

Emile

Dolls house - Mii

Winter   shades

blue

pink

knit

cotton   v v p

Maggie three little kittens (2002),
bisque head and hands, on a cloth
body, limited edition 25.

Nan (2003), on a cloth body, limited edition 30.

Flossie at the seaside (2003), 11.5",
on a wooden body, limited edition 35.

94

Winter Flossie with Toy Shop, limited edition 35.

Two Flossies with pull-a-long animals, limited edition 35.

Flossie with car, limited edition 25.

Annie autumn (2004), 12", on a wooden body, limited edition 35.

Mimi (2004), with train, 10.5", limited edition 35. Also Mimi with Pom-Pom.

Annie and Mimi, limited edition 35,
with gondola, limited edition 25.

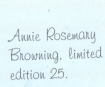

Annie Rosemary
Browning, limited
edition 25.

Mimi in pink (2004), limited edition 35. Christmas Pom-Pom, 8", limited edition 50. Various Pom-Pom.

3) mat ... coat e hat.

4) Jun quit int printed material
e hat ??

5) silk party dress w angura bow.
green
pink

Cat A pygmy lion who loves mice, hates
dogs, and patronizes human beings

Oliver Herford

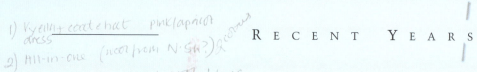

1) Kyenny coat e hat   pink/apricot dress
2) All-in-one (wool from N.Sn?)
3) oth dress nnt   knitted wool blues
    coat e hat.
4) Sun suit nnt printed material hat ??
5) silk party

Cat: A pygmy lion who loves
dogs, and patronizes human

Princess Xenia (2004), on a wooden body. Special edition for Teddy Bears of Witney, limited edition 10.

Henrietta, Violet and Sam.

Ellie.

Top left clockwise, 3 toddlers, Colette large and medium, small Sophy, small Colettes.

Thomas
shirt + waistcoat   — Ann.
knitted trousers   — ~~Miss Harper~~   From.
bed-time set — Janette
boat outfit?   Carolyn.

Laura

Claudine, Poppy and Beth as 3 kings.

Tabitnas outfits 3

new dress   Ann?

Katy with Lily Christmas morning.

At dinner time he would sit in a corner, concentrating,
and suddenly they would say, "Time to feed the cat,"
as if it were their own idea.

Lilian Jackson Braun

106

Laura.

Fleurs.

'Christmas Shopping II', limited edition 17, for The Toy Shoppe.

Lillian dressed in the era of Jane Austen.

DOLL	COPYRIGHT	FIRST YEAR MADE*	LAST YEAR MADE	NUMBER MADE	SPECIAL EDITIONS	BODY TYPE	SIZES
TINY BABY	1982		1989	420		CLOTH A	6"
FLORA	1982		1987	23	PEDDLER, 14" (OOAK)	LEATHER	18"
COLETTE	1982		1986	3		CLOTH B	20"
	1982		1986	23		WOOD A	20"
	1983	1983	1990	50		WOOD	18"
	1982	1983	1989	150	FOR SAVE THE CHILDREN FUND, 35 PIECES	ALL BISQUE	13"
ROSY BABY	1983		1988	52		CLOTH A	12"
		1983	1983	5			
BEECHY HEADS	1983		1984	SMALL, 125 LARGE, 35		BRAN FILLED BODY, WOOD HEAD	
FLORENCE	1984	1984	1991	190		WOOD B	18"
		1985	1990	125		ALL BISQUE	14"
FREDDY (FLORENCE HEAD)		1985	1991	100		WOOD B	18"
		1985	1990	90		ALL BISQUE	14"
MINET-CHERIE	1985	1985	1990	450		CLOTH B	5"
		1986	1990	30	WITH LEATHER TRUNK		
DAISY	1985	1985	1988	30		WOOD B	18"
		1985	1988	40		ALL BISQUE	14"
ALICE	1986	1986	1988	90	WITH TRUNK, 20 PIECES	WOOD A	20"
		1987	1989	100		ALL BISQUE	15"
TODDLERS	1986	1986	1994	AMY, 274. TOM, 205 LUCY, 258. TIM, 177		ALL BISQUE	4.5"
HANNAH	1987	1987	1993	250		WOOD A	20"
		1987	1993	250		WOOD	18"
		1987	1992	440		ALL BISQUE	15"
NEW BABY	1987	1987	1992	230	WITH CRADLE, 50 PIECES	CLOTH B	12"
CLAUDINE	1988	1988	1991	90	CHRISTMAS SHOPPING, 10 PIECES	WOOD A	20"
		1988	1991	90		WOOD A	18"
		1988	1991	200		ALL BISQUE	15"
GEORGY (CLAUDINE HEAD)		1989	1990	12	CHRISTMAS SHOPPING, FOR TOY SHOPPE, 10 PIECES	WOOD	18"
ELIZABETH & JACOB	1988	1989	1989	10	PAIRS, 10 PIECES	ALL WOOD INCLUDING HANDS	28"
BETH	1989	1989	1992	106		WOOD A	20"
		1989	1992	88		WOOD	18"
		1989	1992	340	10TH ANNIVERSARY, 50 PIECES WITH BOX OF TREASURES	ALL BISQUE	15"
POPPY	1989	1989	1994	68	LIMITED EDITION FOR 1990 NEW YORK TOY FAIR IN DARKER VERSION	WOOD A	22"
SOPHY	1990	1990	1994	100	SPECIAL WITH DESK FOR 1991 NEW YORK TOY FAIR	WOOD A	22"
		1990	1994	108	WITH TRAIN, 4 PIECES	WOOD B	18"
		1991	1993	202	CHRISTMAS MORNING, 50 PIECES	ALL BISQUE	12"

DOLL	COPYRIGHT	FIRST YEAR MADE*	LAST YEAR MADE	NUMBER MADE	SPECIAL EDITIONS	BODY TYPE	SIZES
EARLY AMERICAN CHILDREN 2	1990	1990	1992	JANE, 26. EMMA, 34 EDWARD, 18. JAMES, 22		ALL BISQUE	12"
ANNA	1991	1991	1996	113	ANNA & POLLY SET, 4 PIECES (OOAK) FOR 1992 NEW YORK TOY FAIR ANNA & POLLY FOR SUMMER, 2 PIECES INDIAN ANNA 1992 UFDC SAN FRANCISCO, 1 PIECE	WOOD C	20"
POLLY	1991	1991	1996	238	UFDC SAN FRANCICSO	CLOTH	15"
		1993	1994	180			8"
		1993	1994	50	POLLY AT THE SEASIDE WITH TRUNK,		10"
		1993		36	6 PIECES WITH 6 PAINTED SHAKER BOXES		8"
MARY	1992	1992	1994	100	3 PAIRS OF SISTERS FOR 1993 NEW YORK TOY FAIR	WOOD A	18"
	1992	1992	1994	136		ALL BISQUE	15"
EMILY	1992	1992	1994	83	1993 TOY FAIR (SEE MARY ABOVE)	WOOD A	19"
	1992	1992	1994	130		ALL BISQUE	16"
BILLY	1992	1992	1994	23	EDITION WITH CRICKET BAT, 25 PIECES	WOOD A	18"
VIOLET	1993	1993	1995	45	SPECIAL FOR UFDC 1994 CHICAGO,	WOOD A	21"
SAM	1993	1993	1995	26	SMALL VIOLET FOR CEISLIKS PUPPEN MAGAZINE 1994, 6 PIECES	WOOD A	21"
HENRIETTA	1993	1993	1996	183		WOOD A	21"
BABY LILY	1993	1993	1996	REGULAR, 12 ANIMAL BABIES, 53	IN PAINTED BOX, 2 PIECES	CLOTH	7"
BABY AMY	1993	1993	1996	REGULAR, 12. TEDDY, 20 ANIMAL BABIES, 124	IN PAINTED BOX, 6 PIECES	CLOTH	7"
SIMON	1994	1994	1996	30	SPECIAL WITH PUPPET THEATRE FOR UFDC 1995	WOOD A	23"
KATY	1994	1994	1996	63	KATY WITH ARK, 14 PIECES. 15TH ANNIVERSARY KATY 18" WITH TINY FLORENCE, 50 PIECES. KATY, 18", OFF TO THE BEACH, 10 PIECES	WOOD A	20"
JULIETTE (WAX HEAD & SHOULDERS)	1994	1994	1995	15		CLOTH, WAX LIMBS	21"
SUSANNAH	1995	1995	1997	86		WOOD A	20"
LIZZIE	1995	1995	1997	94	PUNCH & JUDY EDITION, 40 PIECES. SPECIAL (OOAK) LIZZIE & PIP GO BOATING, FOR MUSÉE DE LA POUPÉES, PARIS	WOOD A	13.5"
TANSY	1995	1995	1997	72		CLOTH WITH PORCELAIN SHOULDER PLATE, ARMS & LEGS	21"
GABRIELLE	1995	1995	1997	37			21"
LILLIAN	1996	1996	1999	116	SPECIAL (OOAK) FOR NEW YORK TOY FAIR WITH TRUNK, GAINSBOROUGH, 4 PIECES, TISSOT, 6 PIECES, BOTH FOR THE TOY SHOPPE	WOOD A	20"
HEIDI	1996	1996	1998	50	WITH TOY BOX FOR TOY SHOPPE, 25 PIECES	WOOD A WITH JAPANESE PAPIER MÂCHÉ 4" DOLL	13.5"
BABY PIP	1996	1996	1998	100	WITH PRAM, 26 PIECES. FLOWER BABIES, 48 PIECES	CLOTH	10"
MARTHA	1996	1996	1997	LIMITED EDITION USA, 25. EUROPE, 3		WOOD A	18"
FLEUR	1997	1997	1999	63	FLEUR AT THE BALLET, 30 PIECES	WOOD A	17"
TABITHA	1997	1997	1999	73	WITH TOY ELEPHANT, 48 PIECES. CHRISTMAS EDITION, 26 PIECES	CLOTH, ARTICULATED AT HIPS & THIGHS, PORCELAIN HANDS	20"
HOLLY (COLLECTORS CLUB DOLL)	1997	1997		100	18" WOOD BODIED FOR NIADA, 2 PIECES	ALL BISQUE	14"

DOLL	COPYRIGHT	FIRST YEAR MADE*	LAST YEAR MADE	NUMBER MADE	SPECIAL EDITIONS	BODY TYPE	SIZES
LAURA	1998	1998	2000	67	WITH DOLLS HOUSE, 5 PIECES	WOOD A	17"
THOMAS	1998	1998	2002	21	WITH TOY BOAT, 27 PIECES. ARCTIC FOX, 6 PIECES BEDTIME WITH CHLOE, 9 PIECES (SEE BELOW)	CLOTH, LIKE TABITHA	18"
GIGI (COLLECTORS CLUB DOLL)	1998	1998		80		ALL BISQUE	14"
MAY-ROSE	1998	1998	2000	37	1890s FOR THE TOY SHOPPE, 6 PIECES	WOOD A	20"
CHARLOTTE (COLLECTORS CLUB DOLL)	1999	1999		31	SPECIAL FAIRIES, 3 PIECES	CLOTH	14"
JESSICA	1999	1999	2001	23	LITTLE RED RIDING HOOD, 11 PIECES. ALICE, 8 PIECES. GRETEL 8 PIECES. PUSSYCAT, 8 PIECES. HISTORICAL FOR TOY SHOPPE, 8 PIECES 1870s, 7 PIECES. 1770s WITH QUEEN ANN DOLL, 5 PIECES	WOOD A	18"
STEPHEN	1999	1999	2001	5	HANSEL, 8 PIECES, WITH SOAP BOX CART (OOAK, NIADA)	WOOD A	18"
MICHAEL	1999	1999	2001	4	OWL, 8 PIECES	WOOD A	17"
CHLOE	1999	1999	2002	8	LITTLE BO-PEEP, 11 PIECES. MARY-MARY, 10 PIECES WITH THOMAS AS JACK & JILL, 10 PIECES	CLOTH	18"
LYNNE (COLLECTORS CLUB DOLL)	2000	2000		ALL BISQUE, 23 WOOD WITH SCOOTER, 13	CHRISTMAS EDITION FOR THE TOY SHOPPE, 10 PIECES	WOOD ALL BISQUE	18"
ELLIE	2000	2000	2003	69	WITH PRAM, 7 PIECES	WOOD A	19"
LOUISA	2000	2000	2002	33	WITH PRAM, 8 PIECES	WOOD A	19"
CHLOE					CINDERELLA, 9 PIECES. GOLDILOCKS, 20 PIECES THOMAS AS PRINCE CHARMING, 8 PIECES	CLOTH	18"
MOLLY	2000	2000	2003	46	AT SEASIDE, 7 PIECES. ROCK-A-BYE BABY, 4 PIECES FLOWER BABIES, 17 PIECES. WINTER (2001), 22 PIECES	CLOTH	15"
CHLOE					PIRATESS, 4 PIECES. WITH THOMAS AS PIRATE, 4 PIECES SHE SELLS SEA SHELLS, 5 PIECES		
KITTY	2001	2001	2003	58	CAR, 25 PIECES. BOAT, 23 PIECES. PLAYHOUSE, 28 PIECES. CHRISTMAS EDITION FOR THE TOY SHOPPE IN BOX, 12 PIECES		11.5"
DILLY (COLLECTORS CLUB DOLL)	2002				PINK, 60 PIECES. BIRTHDAY SURPRISE, 32 PIECES	CLOTH	7"
DOROTHY	2002	2002	2004	35	DOLLS HOUSE, 35 PIECES. CAR, 25 PIECES. TREE, 30 PIECES CHRISTMAS EDITION FOR TOY SHOPPE, 17 PIECES	WOOD A	11.5"
EMILE	2002	2002		17	WITH SPACESHIP, 10 PIECES	WOOD A	11.5"
MAGGIE	2002	2002		BLUE, 13. WITH PUPPY, 25 WITH 3 LITTLE KITTENS, 24	LIMITED EDITION FOR THERIAULTS, 10 PIECES	CLOTH, FULLY ARTICULATED, BISQUE HANDS	20"
FLOSSIE	2003	2003		CAR, 25. TOY SHOP, 35 PULL-A-LONG DUCK OR BUNNY LIMITED EDITION		WOOD A	11.5"
NAN	2003	2003		FRENCH PROVENCAL, 25 VICTORIAN WINTER GIRLS, 25		CLOTH, SAME AS MAGGIE BUT OLDER	18"
ANNIE	2004			WITH TRUNK, 25. AUTUMN, 35 WITH POODLE, 35		WOOD A	12"
MIMI	2004			WITH TRAIN, 35. POODLE, 35, IN PINK, 35	DOLLS WITH POODLES & GONDOLA, LIMITED EDITION, 25 PIECES	WOOD A	10.5"
BABY POM-POM	2004					CLOTH	7"

* year before they appear in catalogue

KEY
OOAK – One of a kind

114

LIST OF COPIES MADE.

SFBJ 236	1980/81	7
STEINER C	1980/85	27
JUMEAU E.J.*	1980/85	35
JUMEAU TÊTE DÉPOSÉE *	1980/81	40
GOOGLY	1980/82	9
SMALL BRU	1980/88	51
SMALL JUMEAU LONG FACE	1980/85	25
LARGE A.T.	1980/85	43
K. R. 114 *	1980/88	187
LARGE SFBJ 252	1980/82	9
LARGE BRU JNE	1980/86	29
KESTNER BABY	1980/86	87
SMALL FRENCH ALL BISQUE	1980	87
GERMAN ORIENTAL *	1980/84	11
KLEY AND HAHN	1980	1
SMALL A.M. DREAM BABY *	1981/86	321
SFBJ 227 *	1981/85	11
KESTNER XI	1981	3
K.R. 100 *	1981	1
PORTRAIT JUMEAU *	1981/85	8
BYE-LO BABY	1981/85	54
K.R. 117 *	1982/87	40
GERMAN TWO FACED DOLL *	1982	1
SMALL A.T.*	1982/84	7
BÉBÉ F.G.*	1982/84	9
LARGE JUMEAU LONG FACE	1982/85	17
LARGE A.M. DREAM BABY *	1982/89	48
LARGE BROWN A.M. DREAM BABY *		1
A.M. 560	1982/83	5
MEDIUM BRU *	1983/85	9
SMALL JUMEAU E.J. *	1983/87	52
SMALL BÉBÉ SCHMITT	1983/89	34
LARGE BRU	1983/85	11
HORSEMAN BABY	1983/88	296
SFBJ 252	1983/88	399
FRENCH FASHION LADY KIT *	1984/87	73
K.R. 109 *	1984/85	5
LARGE KESTNER BABY	1984	1
VERY SMALL BRU	1984/86	16
S.& H. 719 *	1985/89	40
TINY A.M. DREAM BABY *	1985/86	31
GOOGLY	1985/87	17

* Those marked with an asterisk were made using their own moulds

Ellie

Susannah & Lizzie

Kitty

Cloth Nan

Cloth Tabitha & Thomas

Jessica & Michael

Group of earlier wood bodies

L – R, large Beth, medium Beth, large Sophy, medium Sophy & Anna

Articles in magazines & exhibition catalogues

'Lynne und Michael Roche' by Rudolf Ebeling in Puppenmagazin no 4, 1988.

'Poupées, créations d'hier et d'aujourd'hui': catalogue: exhibition held in summer 1988, in Musée de Poupées, Josselin, France.

'The Dolls of Lynne and Michael Roche' by Lauran Stevens in Doll Reader, April 1989.

'Artists and Inspiration: Lynne and Michael Roche' by Lauran Stevens, Cover Story in Doll Artistry, August to September 1991.

'Poupées d'hier, Créations d'aujourd'hui': catalogue: exhibition held April to November 1991, in Musée des Arts Décoratifs, Palais du Louvre, Paris, France.

'From Concept to Reality' by Barbara Spadaccini-Day in Dolls, October 1991.

'Timeless Contemporaries by Lynne and Michael Roche' by Krystyna Poray-Goddu, Cover Story in Dolls, July 1992.

'And Is There Honey Still For Tea?' by John Darcy Noble in Contemporary Doll Magazine, November 1992.

'Doll Art, Internationale Puppenszene', catalogue: exhibition 'Doll Art 1994', Frankfurt, May, 1994.

'Making it together' by Lauran Stevens, Cover story in Doll Magazine, Winter 1994/95.

'La Poupée d'Aujourd'hui, un Art Vivant,' exhibition catalogue, Bibliothèque Forney, Paris, January to April, 1998.

Selected Pieces of Sekiguichi Doll Garden. District of Izu, Japan, 1998.

'Das stille Glück der Kindertage' by Silke Heller, Cover story in Puppen & Spielzeug, April 1999.

Books

The Ultimate Doll Book, Caroline Goodfellow, Dorling Kindersley, London, G.B., 1993.

World Guide to Dolls, Valerie Jackson Douet, The Apple Press, London, G.B., 1993.

La Poupée d'Aujourd'hui, Un art Vivant, Ingebord Riesser, Editions Massin, Paris, France, 1996.

Dolls, A Collector's Guide, Olivia Bristol, De Agostini Editions, London, G.B., 1997.

15th Blue Book, Jan Foulke, Hooby House Press, U.S.A., 2001.

The World's Most Beautiful Dolls, Joan Muyskens Pursley, Karin Bischoff , Portfolio Press, U.S.A., 1994.

The World's Most Beautiful Dolls, vol 2, Joan Muyskens Pursley, Portfolio Press, U.S.A., 2001.

Exhibitions

'Poupées, créations d'hier et d'aujourd'hui': Summer 1988, Musée de Poupées, Josselin, France.

'Poupées d'hier, Créations d'aujourd'hui': April to November 1991, Musée des Arts Décoratifs, Palais du Louvre, Paris, France. This exhibition was then on display in museums in Bordeaux, Bourges, Melun and Lunéville throughout 1992 and 1993.

Doll Art, Frankfurt, Germany, 1994 to 1998.

'Poupées d'Artistes, collection Ingebord Riesser,': May to September 1995, Château de Meillant, France.

Solo exhibition in Gillian Still's Gallery, Llandeilo, Wales, November 1995.

'Une Dimanche à la Campagne': October – November 1996, Musée de la Poupée, Paris.

'La Poupée d'Aujourd'hui, un Art Vivant': January to April, 1998, Bibliothèque Forney, Paris.

'Barbarella, dolls and doll imagery': July to August, 1998, Folkston G.B. Then this exhibition traveled around Great Britain until June 1999.

Sekiguichi Doll Garden Museum, Ito-Shi, Japan. For opening 1998 and permanent collection.

'De la literature au jeux video: Poupées et Personnages Mythiques': June to October 2004, Musée de Poupées, Josselin, France.

Her interest in contemporary creation and artist dolls started in 1980 when she first came into contact with the work of Anne Mitrani (France) and a little later, the dolls created by Lynne and Michael Roche, through photographs of Freddy and Florence.

From 1981 until recently retiring in 2003, she worked in the Decorative Arts Museum in Paris, Palais du Louvre, as assistant-curator, then curator of the Toy Department, where she was responsible for some 12000 toys – antique and contemporary – ranging from dolls, teddy bears, board games, cars, boats, trains, to dolls houses.

In conjunction with her work as curator, she has planned and set up many exhibitions in the museum as well as travelling with these exhibitions to museums all over France, Monaco, Switzerland and Japan.

In addition to her work at the Decorative Arts Museum, Barbara Spadaccini-Day has had an ongoing collaboration with Antionette de Rohan, at le Musée de Poupées in Josselin Brittany, since its opening in 1984.

The extent of her interest is wide and varied. It started in the early 1970s with French antique dolls. This developed into a global knowledge of the French toy industry, past and present.

Research is her forte. Since the early 1980s she has written for specialized magazines in the United States, Great Britain, France and Australia – Dolls, Doll Reader, Doll News, Teddy Bear and Friends, Toy and Doll – as well as articles in exhibition catalogues, and prefacing books of doll artists in Japan. She researched and wrote an in-depth historical perspective on Jules Nicolas Steiner, a 19th century French doll maker, for D. McGonagle's book.

In 1992 Barbara was invited to Canada as scientifique counsellor to several museums; Glenbow, Calgary and Vancover.

Barbara is also a member of UFDC, a NIADA patron, and past president of CERP (France), she participates in conventions with presentations and articles for their journals.

Barbara Spadaccini-Day holds a University Degree in the French University of Paris XIII on the 'Science of Play'.

Barbara has a double nationality – English and French. Born in England, she spent her adolescent years in Australia, and her married life in France, where she lives.

She confesses to a longstanding admiration for the work of Lynne and Michael Roche.

Bold type refers to illustrations. OOAK – abbreviation of 'one of a kind'

Bold type refers to illustrations. OOAK – abbreviation of 'one of a kind'